ENERGY FILES
COAL

ENERGY FILES – COAL
was produced by

David West ☂☂ Children's Books
7 Princeton Court
55 Felsham Road
London SW15 1AZ

Editor: James Pickering
Picture Research: Carrie Haines, Carlotta Cooper

First published in Great Britain in 2002 by
Heinemann Library, Halley Court, Jordan Hill,
Oxford OX2 8EJ, a division of Reed Educational
and Professional Publishing Limited.

OXFORD MELBOURNE AUCKLAND
JOHANNESBURG BLANTYRE GABORONE
IBADAN PORTSMOUTH (NH) USA CHICAGO

06 05 04 03 02
10 9 8 7 6 5 4 3 2 1

ISBN 0 431 15572 0 (HB)
ISBN 0 431 15579 8 (PB)

British Library Cataloguing in Publication Data

Parker, Steve, 1952 -
Coal. - (Energy files)
1. Coal - Juvenile literature
I. Title
333.8'22

Printed and bound in Italy

PHOTO CREDITS :
Abbreviations: t-top, m-middle, b-bottom, r-right,
l-left, c-centre.

Front cover all - Corbis Images. 3, 4-5 both, 7r,
10bl, 10-11b, 11bl, 13b, 16-17t, 17t & m, 20bl,
20-21, 21tr, 22 both, 23bl & br, 24br, 27bl, 28bl,
29tr - Corbis Images. 5br (Mark Edwards), 14-15,
15bl, 16-17b (Peter Frischmuth), 15br (F. & A.
Mitchler), 19br, 26mr (Thomas Raupach), 21tl
(Shehzad Nooran), 21ml (A. Maclean - Peter
Arnold Inc.), 25tr (Sabine Vielmo) - Still Pictures.
6bl - Mary Evans Picture Library. 6mr, 13tl -
Spectrum Colour Library. 6-7 (Gavin Hellier), 8tr
(H.P. Merten), 8b, 19tr (Tony Waltham), 9mr
(Carolina Biological Supp/Phototake NYC), 9bm
(David Hughes), 13mr (G. & P. Corrigan), 18bl
(Walter Rawlings), 18-19t (Robert Francis), 24bl
(Tony Gervuis), 29tl (Tomlinson), 24-25 - Robert
Harding Picture Library. 14 both - Katz/FSP. 17br -
Dover Books. 27br - Sasol Limited. 30mr -
University of Southampton.

*An explanation of difficult words can be
found in the glossary on page 31.*

ENERGY FILES
COAL

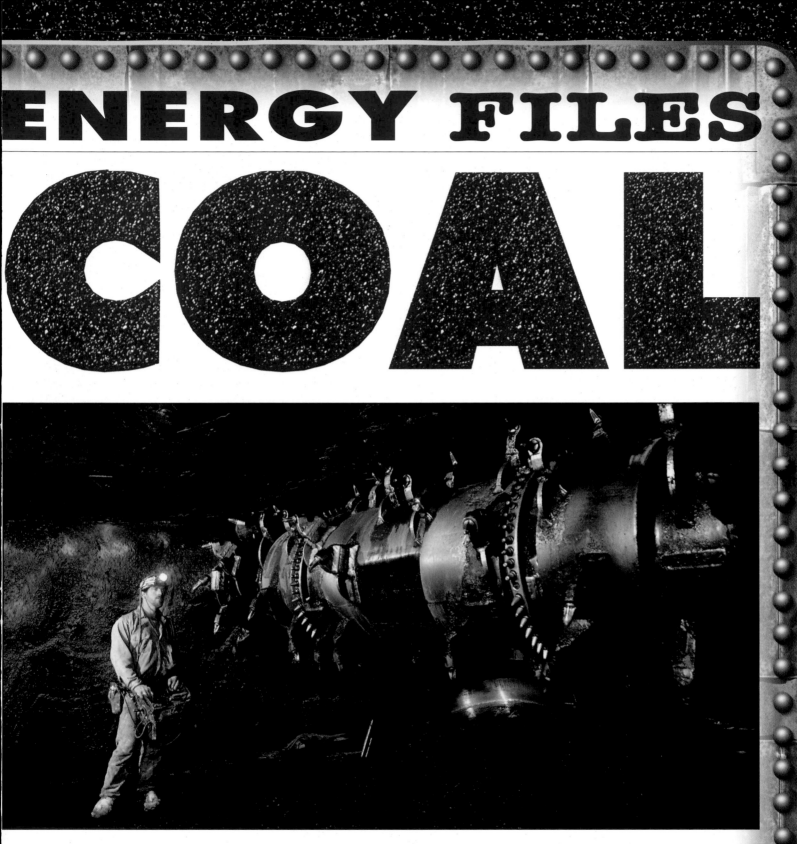

Steve Parker

Heinemann
LIBRARY

CONTENTS

Coal can be burned – or it can be used as a raw material for a huge range of products, from powerful acid chemicals to gentle soaps.

These tall towers house the winding pulleys for the lifts in a coal mine. Miners' lives hang by a cable as they descend into the depths.

INTRODUCTION

Few rocks from the Earth are as useful as coal. This hard, black substance is valued worldwide as a source of energy – heat. We burn coal in power stations, factory furnaces, railway steam locomotives, and in the stove or fireplace at home. People still risk their lives mining coal, deep underground. Great industries have been built on the power yielded by burning coal. But this causes many kinds of pollution, and like all fossil fuels, coal supplies cannot last for ever.

Hundreds of tonnes of coal wait in railroad wagons (below), for their journey to an electricity power station (inset). Yet even this enormous quantity is only a few days' supply for the power station furnaces.

THE COAL AGE

Pick up a lump of coal, and you touch a long-gone time, even before dinosaurs roamed the Earth. Most coal formed hundreds of millions of years ago, mainly during the Carboniferous Period – the 'Age of Coal Forests'.

WARM AND WET

During Carboniferous times, 360–286 million years ago, the world was warm and damp, like a tropical rainforest today. Giant ferns, horsetails and other ancient plants grew in vast, steamy swamps, marshes and bogs. It was well before any dinosaurs. Animals in the coal swamps included newt-like amphibians as big as crocodiles and crow-sized dragonflies. Lush green plants lived, died, piled up in the warm shallow water, and gradually turned to coal (see page 8).

Many lumps of coal contain the fossilized shapes of prehistoric life such as ferns and insects.

There were no flowers, grasses or broadleaved trees in the Carboniferous Period. The main big plants were ferns, tree-ferns, horsetails, conifers and club-mosses.

Peat is an early stage in coal formation. People burn peat to heat their homes, and use it to help grow crops, but it is in short supply.

MORE AGES OF COAL

Whenever warm, wet conditions have existed in Earth's history, coal has slowly formed. Other main coal-forest periods include the Permian (286–250 million years ago), Triassic (250–206), Jurassic (206–144), Cretaceous (144–65) and Tertiary (65–2). Dinosaurs lived during the middle three of these periods. But more than half of all coal used today is from the Carboniferous age.

Coal for the FUTURE?

Warm, damp conditions exist in certain regions today, and encourage the growth of swampy forests, with moss-draped cypress trees and creeping vines. But these will not become coal until millions of years in the future. The rate of coal formation today is almost zero.

Temperate rainforest in Washington State, USA.

HOW COAL FORMED

Coal is not just coal. There are various types, of different colours and hardness. They release different amounts of heat energy when burned. This is because coal formation is a continuous process.

EARLY STAGES

Making coal needs four conditions: plants, pressure, temperature and time. In an ancient coal forest, plants did not rot away or get eaten. They died and lay in shallow water, where the process of decay was very slow. Gradually the layers deepened …

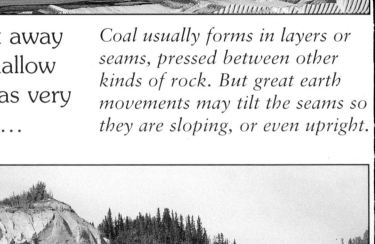

A lignite (brown coal) mine near Cologne, Germany. Lignite burns slowly with a yellow, smoky flame, so it is not often used for fires and stoves in homes.

Coal usually forms in layers or seams, pressed between other kinds of rock. But great earth movements may tilt the seams so they are sloping, or even upright.

Coal can be viewed as rock, a fossil or a mineral. Its formation began with plants that decayed very slowly. They became buried, pressed and squashed. As more layers collected above, the plant remains were buried deeper, where the rocks were hotter. Each stage produced a different type of coal. Anthracite is hardest, darkest and gives off most heat.

Living forest

Plants thrived in warm dampness, died and piled up in deep layers.

Peat

Part-buried plants partly rot into a moist, fibrous, spongy mass.

Lignite

This type of coal is dry and woody, with bits of the original plants still visible.

Bituminous coal

Most ordinary coal is bituminous – fairly hard, with a sheen and layered texture.

Anthracite

Very hard, black and glossy, this type burns hottest and with the least smoke or soot.

Dangerous STUFF

Anthracite is the purest form of coal, containing the greatest energy. Lump for lump, it is more valuable than other coals – and even more than many other rocks and minerals. It can occur at great depths, and people may take great risks, and even break laws, to mine it.

Anthracite – 'black gold'?

ENERGY CONTENT

The heat energy released by burning coal – or any other substance – is measured in kilojoules per gram. Lignite contains up to 15 (about the same as meat in our food), bituminous coal 20–35, and anthracite usually over 30.

Ordinary household coal is usually bituminous.

WHERE COAL IS FOUND

Coal is found on every main continent (land-mass) in the world. More than half the world's countries have some supplies. But they vary greatly in amount and quality, and how difficult it is to mine the coal from the ground, and transport it to where it's needed.

FOSSIL FUEL

Coal is a fossil fuel – it was formed long ago from once-living things. There are about one million million tonnes of known coal supplies. Surveyors and geologists (rock specialists) continually search for more.

NORTH AMERICA

SOUTH AMERICA

Coal-mining areas

A surveyor measures hills and valleys in the landscape, looking for tell-tale signs of coal under the surface.

WORLD SUPPLIES

Supplies of coal are widely spread around the world. But many of these stores, or reserves, are small amounts. Others are in remote places or very deep below the surface, so they are costly to mine. More than half of all the world's known supplies are in three nations – Russia, USA and China. These places are also the biggest users of coal. New reserves are being discovered especially in South America, Africa and Australia.

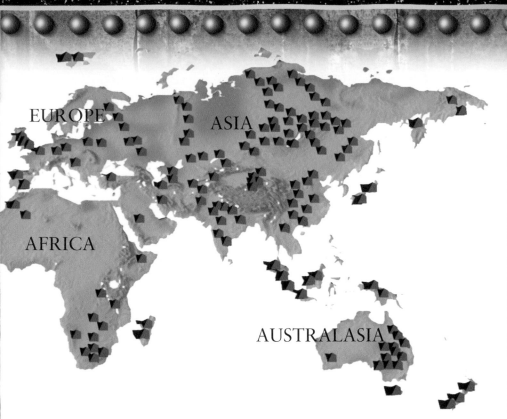

EUROPE

ASIA

AFRICA

AUSTRALASIA

HOW MUCH IS LEFT?

If we use coal in the future, at the rate we use it today, the known amounts of coal in the world should last 200 years. This is three or four times longer than the other two main fossil fuels, oil (petroleum) and natural gas. Probably, more coal waits to be discovered, and mining methods continue to improve.

Green ISSUES

Coal is big business, with fortunes to be made. Mining companies look for new supplies. But mines can scar the land and harm wildlife. There are heated arguments about mining companies exploring natural wilderness areas such as Alaska and Antarctica.

Nature under threat?

Geologists use a test-drilling rig to remove a rod-like core of rock, and examine it for coal.

COAL MINES

Over the ages, great earth movements bend, fold, bury and raise rock layers – including coal seams. So coal is found at all levels, from the surface to thousands of metres below. If there is enough good-quality coal in an area, then it is dug out by mining.

Green ISSUES

When the coal ran out, many old mines were simply left. They flooded, or soil and rocks gradually collapsed into the shafts and chambers below. This subsidence makes an area extremely dangerous.

THE COAL MINE

Coal is cut by machines from the coal face (see page 16). Roof supports stop rocks collapsing into the empty space left. The coal is carried by conveyor or small trucks to a huge bunker, where it is measured into a large coal skip. The skip is pulled up the mine shaft by cables in the winding house, emptied, and sent back for its next load. A surface conveyor takes the coal to railway wagons.

Coal train

Loading tower

Surface conveyor

Winding house

Washing and sorting

Coal face

Coal cutter

Roof supports

Conveyor

Storage bunker

Mine shaft

Coal skip

The ground over a disused mine can give way at any time.

Even in the middle of the night, the mine works at full speed. The winding house has large pulleys inside which hold the cables for the coal skips and people elevators. Sloping conveyors carry coal for washing and sorting in tall towers.

NON-STOP MINING

A modern coal mine runs non-stop. The cut coal is carried on moving belts called conveyors to skips, and hauled up wide concrete shafts. More conveyors at the surface take it up into towers, where it is washed, and sorted or graded, then tipped into railway wagons. Much mining machinery is automatic.

Not all coal mines are as automated as those in the West.

WORKING IN A MINE

Long ago, coal was chipped with hand-axes and carried in bags. This back-breaking work has disappeared in nearly all mines today. But the miner's job is still hard, tiring and uncomfortable. And, despite enormous safety improvements, accidents can happen.

Miners descend in cage-like elevators (lifts). One group, or shift, replaces a previous shift.

HOT AND DUSTY

Some mines go down more than 1,500 metres. At these depths the rocks are very warm. Air is filtered and freshened by pumps, but it is still hot and humid. The machines are noisy, the lights glare, and black coal dust seems to get everywhere.

All miners have a hard-hat and light, in case the general light system fails. An unlit mine is totally black.

As a mine spreads, new conveyors and rails are put into tunnels and chambers where coal once was – or dug into solid rock.

In a big mine, workers may have to ride several kilometres from the shaft to the coal face, in small underground trains.

ALL ELECTRIC

Machines and lights in a mine are electric. Petrol or diesel engines would use valuable oxygen that miners need to breathe, and give off deadly fumes. Air is filtered to remove poisonous or explosive gases that seep naturally from some kinds of rocks. In many mines there is an endless battle to pump out water, which trickles in from the rocks all around.

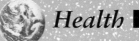

Health RISKS

Coal dust floats in the air in a mine. When miners do not use masks or filters, they breathe it in. The dust particles clog the body's airways and lungs and cause wheezing, shortness of breath, coughs, colds, and chest illnesses with the general name of 'miner's lung'. In some cases the dust can trigger changes which result in deadly forms of lung cancer.

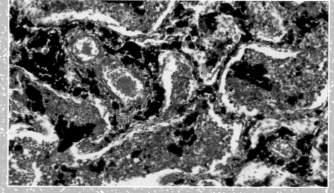

'Miner's lung' seen through a microscope.

CUTTING COAL

Coal may be softer than some rocks. But it is still a rock, and very hard. A big mine may cut a million tonnes of coal each year out of the ground.

SEAMS AND SHEARERS

In most mines, coal is in layers or seams. People first find seams using hand-controlled cutters, hydraulic hammers or even explosives. When a long length of seam is available, a shearer can move along it, cutting off lumps as it goes. This is called longwall mining.

THE LONGWALL

Longwall mining uses a wheel with teeth called a shearer or cutter. This spins slowly as it is pulled along by a chain and pressed against the coal seam. The teeth chop bits off the 'long wall' of coal, which are guided on to the conveyor.

Some cutters bore a hole in the coal face like a huge drill, while others scratch and bite against the exposed surface.

A shearer's teeth or blades have tips of very hard metal or even tiny diamonds.

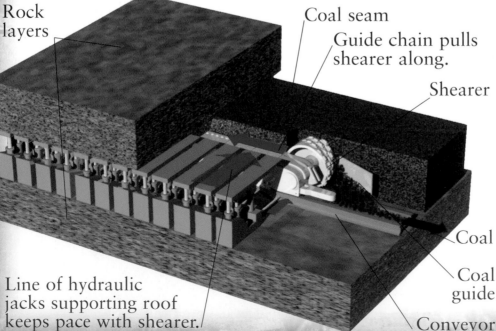

Rock layers

Coal seam

Guide chain pulls shearer along.

Shearer

Coal

Coal guide

Line of hydraulic jacks supporting roof keeps pace with shearer.

Conveyor

PILLAR-AND-ROOM

As coal is taken away, it leaves empty space or 'room'. The pillar-and-room system leaves columns of coal to hold the rock layer above, saving the cost of roof supports. Pillars may be cut last, as miners work their way back out.

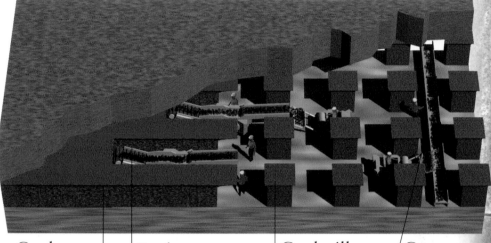

Coal seam | Coal cutters | Coal pillars | Conveyor

Holes are drilled into the seam for sticks of explosive. Loud hooters warn that a blast is due – noise and air pressure in the limited space would be very harmful.

MORE MINING METHODS

The longwall shearer breaks the coal and loads it straight on to a conveyor or into trucks. But in some mines, the seams are too short or curved. There are many other ways to cut the coal, such as jack-hammers resembling road-drills, undercutters similar to huge chainsaws, and drilling for explosives to blast off lumps.

Old-time MINES

Only 100 years ago, mining was an extremely risky business. Workers used picks and shovels, and wooden pit props held up the roof. The air was foul, and the naked flame of candle lamps could cause explosions.

A 19th-century coal mine.

COAL AT THE SURFACE

More than half of all coal is not dug deep underground, but taken from the surface, by open-cast mining. This type of mine relies on giant diggers and excavators, bigger than houses.

STRIP MINING

Open-cast mining is often called strip mining. In most cases, the digging takes place along a ribbon-like strip. Each strip is prepared by scraping off the soil and thin layers of covering rock, which are called the 'overburden'. The soil is stockpiled, or stored, to be put back later. Then the huge diggers move in, with roads for trucks, or a conveyor that is extended longer and longer, to carry the coal away.

Some mines have their own power stations. Electricity is easier to transport than coal.

STRIP MINE

The swing-arm cutter bites off an arc of coal, and then crawls a short distance on its tracks, to do the same again. When the strip is mined out, it is filled in with the rock overburden which is being removed from the next strip, while the soil is put back over the previous strip.

Original top soil replaced

Crops grown on reclaimed land

Bucket excavators scrape away the top soil. In some open-cast mines they are also used to scoop out soft types of coal.

Green ISSUES

Early strip mines (from about 1910) left vast gaping holes. These still remain as terrible scars on a ruined landscape. Today a mined area must be reclaimed, or put back to a suitable condition. It may be used for farming, sports like golf, flooded as a leisure lake, or combined with rubbish disposal as a landfill site.

Earth's wounds take centuries to 'heal'.

Next strip of top soil and rock to be removed

Some swing-arm excavators or cutters have teeth that crumble the coal on to a conveyor. Others have a series of buckets that lift the coal up and over, on to a conveyor in the arm.

Excavators

Coal seam

Conveyor

Rock layer from strip being mined put on previous strip

Swing-arm cutter

CARRYING COAL

In many regions the great centres of industry, with factories and workers, use vast amounts of coal for power and as raw material. Yet the coal itself is mined thousands of kilometres away, and has to be transported. Why?

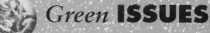
RESULT OF HISTORY

Coal has affected recent history. Many of today's industrial centres were set up near mines. Coal fuelled furnaces and cities grew. But those mines have run out. Now the coal must come from far away.

A coal train rumbles along, carrying coal from a remote mine to a power station in North America. These trains can be 100 wagons long, with each wagon capable of carrying up to 100 tonnes of coal.

Many power stations are on river banks or by the sea. Water is needed by the power station, for cooling. And cargo ships or massive barges can moor alongside, bringing coal for the power station burners.

Scavenging for coal.

Coal stockpiles cope with sudden surges in demand.

CHOOSING TRANSPORT

Coal is one of the bulkiest, heaviest kinds of cargo. To transport it by air or road would cost more than the coal itself is worth. So carrying coal is a slow, steady business, suited to transport which uses energy efficiently – railway wagons, ships and barges. Storage is also vital, giving spare coal for urgent local needs.

COAL BY SEA

As new mines open, new transport routes take coal to existing industrial regions. Each year 400 million tonnes go by sea. For example, new industries in South East Asia, with few mines, are fuelled partly by Australian coal.

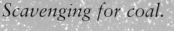

NORTH AMERICA
EUROPE
SOUTH EAST ASIA
SOUTH AMERICA
SOUTH AFRICA
AUSTRALIA

21

COAL FOR POWER

The main use of coal is for power – electrical power. About half of the world's coal is burned to produce a third of the world's electricity. The power station releases the chemical energy locked up in coal.

HOW GENERATORS WORK

Turbines and generators are found in most power stations. Pressurized steam blasts against the turbine's angled blades, spinning their shaft. This is also the shaft of huge wire coils, the rotor, which spins in the magnetism made by the stator around it. When a wire moves in a magnetic field, electricity flows, and is led away from the rotor.

COAL-FIRED POWER STATION

Coal burns better and hotter if it is pulverized into a powder. This is mixed with fresh air which has been pre-heated as it passed the waste hot gases from the boiler.

In the boiler, water is superheated to steam which is led to the turbines. The boiler gases are cleaned or 'scrubbed' before leaving the smokestack.

1 Coal is cleaned and scrubbed.

Main boiler

Air intake

6 Hot gases warm incoming air.

Smoke stack

Coal ramp

Coal hopper

2 Coal is powdered in hot air.

3 Powdered coal and air blow into boiler.

4 Water in pipes is heated to high-pressure steam.

5 Steam spins turbines.

GENERATOR

Stator produces
magnetic field.

Rotor

Electricity   Shaft

TURBINE

Blades

Steam

Used steam to
cooling tower

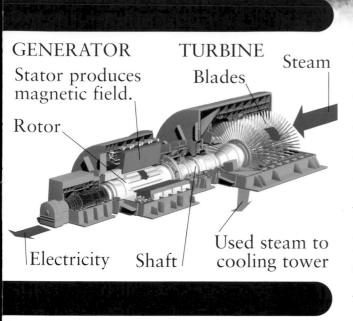

Some cooling towers have their own
water pipes to collect 'spare' heat,
which warms nearby buildings.

Cooling tower

7 Used steam   8 Cooled water goes
goes to tower.   back to main boiler.

BETTER IN SOME WAYS

Even in a modern power station,
less than half the energy in coal is
converted into electrical energy.
Scientists and engineers constantly
search for new ways to make the
process more efficient, but at the same
time, reduce the terrible burden of
pollution and harm to the environment.
Coal is the 'dirtiest' of the main fuels
used in power stations (see page 28).

Green ISSUES

To some people, fumes from a power
station smokestack (chimney) are a small
side-effect from a great triumph of modern
engineering, which provides electricity to
drive today's world. To others, the fumes are
wasted heat and harmful polluting gases.

Better filters 'scrub' fumes cleaner.

COAL IN INDUSTRY

About a quarter of the world's coal is used to provide heat energy for industry. It is burned in furnaces, boilers, ovens, stoves, forges, kilns and smelters.

THE HEAT IS ON

All these types of coal-burners release heat for industrial processes. Some important products which need plenty of heat to make are iron, steel, glass, cement, plastics, rubber, pottery, various chemicals – and bread, pies and cakes!

At a steel works, coke fuel burns at more than 1,600°C to melt the metal into a liquid.

Coal is still used in some regions for travel and transport, to fire the boilers of steam locomotives.

Green ISSUES

One of the great problems facing the world is global warming, due to climate change (see page 28). Burning fossil fuels such as coal makes the 'greenhouse gases' like carbon dioxide that contribute to the problem. The answer: burn less of everything, including coal.

Carbon dioxide (CO_2) is given off by burning.

Over many industrial towns, the skies fill with smoke, soot and fumes from coal-fired furnaces and boilers.

PROCESSING COAL

For some industries, ordinary coal does not burn at suitable temperatures. So it is changed to other forms. For example, it can be heated at 1,200°C without air to make coke, or slow-fired in little air to make charcoal. These products burn at much higher temperatures. Coke is used in blast furnaces to make iron and steel.

FLUIDIZED BED

In fluidized bed combustion, ground-up coal and limestone burn in a very hot furnace of sand, which 'boils' like a liquid. Water is heated to steam for one turbine, exhaust gases drive another turbine, and there is less overall pollution.

Gases to turbine

Steam to turbine

Floating bed of fluid sand

Coal and limestone

Water

Air

25

Not all coal is burned for heat energy. Some is treated by a process called gasification. This makes various gases, which are used in three main ways – as raw materials for industry, to burn for heat, or to drive gas turbines.

COAL OILS AND TARS

Gasifying coal, and heating it to make coke, produces 'leftovers' such as thick, gooey tars. Also the gases from gasification can be cooled and turned into coal oils and similar liquids. These coal tars and oils have many uses. They are processed to make fertilizers, solvents, preservatives like creosote and pitch, chemicals for industry, coloured dyes and even soap!

In a coking plant, the gases and vapours given off are cooled to form various oils, liquids and tars, called fractions.

Green ISSUES

Like any heavy industry, processing coal makes by-products and wastes. Coal slurry may escape into waterways and damage wildlife. Certain coal tar products and solvents are now known to be harmful – a few may cause cancers, and so must be treated with great care.

A 'black tide' of coal slurry.

Coal-tar soap has a unique aroma and a reputation for getting skin and hair very clean. A distinctive smell also comes from mothballs, which contain the substance naphthalene, another of coal's many chemical products.

COAL GASIFIER

In a gasifier, coal is brought into contact with steam and the gas oxygen. The coal does not actually burn or combust. But at such a high temperature and pressure, its chemical substances break apart or 'crack' into smaller, lighter substances, especially gas fuels. These can be bottled or stored and burned later. The heat energy in the gasifier boils water into steam, which is used by turbines to generate electricity in the usual way.

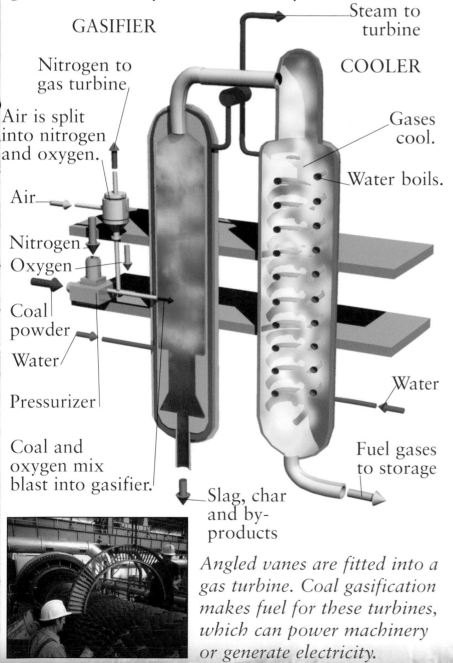

GASIFIER

Nitrogen to gas turbine

Air is split into nitrogen and oxygen.

Air

Nitrogen

Oxygen

Coal powder

Water

Pressurizer

Coal and oxygen mix blast into gasifier.

Steam to turbine

COOLER

Gases cool.

Water boils.

Water

Fuel gases to storage

Slag, char and by-products

Angled vanes are fitted into a gas turbine. Coal gasification makes fuel for these turbines, which can power machinery or generate electricity.

BETTER RESULTS

Overall, gasifying coal to make fuel gases, which are then burned, can make less pollution than burning the coal itself. Also, the gasifying process yields useful raw materials. In new 'hybrid' systems, coal is first gasified, and the leftovers are then burned. This can obtain more than half of the heat energy locked up in the coal.

This South African chemical factory makes the substance AO-octene partly from coal. AO-octene is then used to produce thin, see-through plastic 'cling-film' wrapping sheets.

POLLUTION BY COAL

In the last century, cities like London choked with smoke and fumes from coal-fired furnaces, power stations and millions of home fires. People died, and new laws were introduced. Today there is less smoke and soot, but coal still causes much pollution.

 Green **ISSUES**

Air pollution comes from many sources, not only from burning coal, but from vehicle exhausts and chemical factories. It may be partly to blame for a steep rise in breathing problems such as asthma.

THE GREENHOUSE EFFECT

As our world becomes more industrial, burning more coal and other fuels, the levels of carbon dioxide (CO_2) in the atmosphere rise. Like the glass in a greenhouse, this gas makes the atmosphere trap more of the Sun's heat, rather than letting it pass back into space, and the world gets warmer.

CO_2 builds up in atmosphere.

Energy is reflected back into space.

Energy from Sun

Some heat escapes the atmosphere.

Burning coal, oil, gas, wood and similar fuels all produce carbon dioxide. Coal also gives off other pollutants.

Burning fossil fuels release CO_2.

Extra heat trapped by greenhouse gases increases temperature of atmosphere.

Inhalers ease asthma wheezing.

Acid rain damages trees, seeps into rivers and lakes, kills fish – all this occurs far away from the polluter.

GLOBAL WARMING

Burning almost any fuel, including coal, produces carbon dioxide. It collects in the atmosphere, causing heat to build up by the greenhouse effect. The result, global warming, may affect world climates, melt polar ice-caps, raise sea levels, flood low-lying land and disrupt farming, weather and wildlife. The solution: burn less, save energy.

ACID RAIN

Fumes from coal-fired power stations contain many chemicals. Some of these rise into the air and dissolve in the water in clouds, making it acid. Filters or scrubbers in chimneys and smokestacks can reduce the problem. But the main solution is: burn less, save energy.

HOW ACID RAIN FORMS

Chemicals in the fumes from burning coal include sulphur and nitrogen oxides. These drift high in the air and dissolve in tiny water droplets in clouds, making the water acidic. The droplets merge and fall as rain which harms plants, animals and the soil.

Sulphur and nitrogen from burning fossil fuels

Acid rain falls far away.

Wind

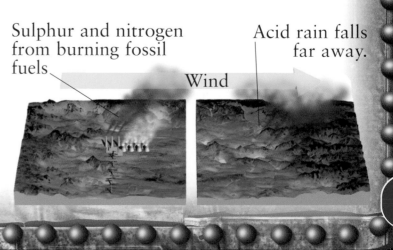

FUTURE COAL ENERGY

There is enough coal in the world to last for another two centuries. But pollution problems are huge now. And what will happen when coal runs out?

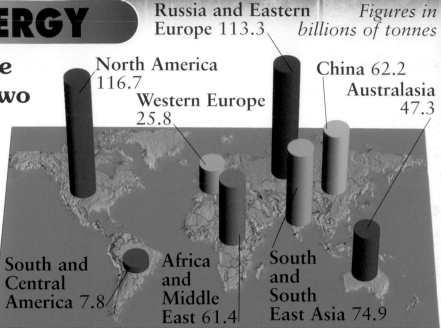

Figures in billions of tonnes

Russia and Eastern Europe 113.3

North America 116.7

China 62.2

Australasia 47.3

Western Europe 25.8

South and Central America 7.8

Africa and Middle East 61.4

South and South East Asia 74.9

CLEAN AND EFFICIENT

Coal will stay as a valuable energy source for years to come. Also, ways of getting the energy from it will improve, such as using coal slurry to make the gas hydrogen for fuel cells.

The world has 500 billion tonnes of coal to mine with today's methods, and more with future technology.

COAL TO HYDROGEN

Coal slurry combined with calcium oxide ('quicklime') produces the gas hydrogen and calcium carbonate ('limestone'). Hydrogen powers fuel cells that generate electricity, and heat recycles the calcium substances.

Electricity

Coal and calcium produce hydrogen.

Coal slurry

Fuel cells

Heat is used to recycle calcium.

Carbon dioxide

Calcium chemicals

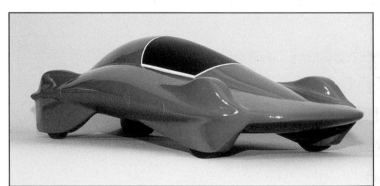

Could steam-powered supercars like this, fuelled by coal, carry us into the future?

THE END WILL COME

However, one day coal will run out. The distant future lies in renewable, low-pollution energy sources, and saving energy all round.

GLOSSARY

combust
Burn, combining with oxygen and giving off a large amount of heat and light.

dissolve
Spread as tiny particles through a liquid called the solvent. A dissolved substance seems to disappear, but it is still there.

gasify
Turn a solid substance into gases or vapours, by heating.

global warming
The rise in temperature all around the world, due to greenhouse gases (see below) in the layer of air, or atmosphere. They trap extra amounts of the Sun's heat.

greenhouse gases
Substances in the atmosphere (air) which hold in or retain the Sun's heat. They keep it near to Earth's surface, rather than letting it escape into space, causing global warming (see above).

overburden
The soil and rocks lying on top of a seam of coal near the surface.

renewable
A process or substance that can continue for a very long time, using raw materials or resources that are recycled or made again.

scrubbing
In a power station, filtering and cleaning the fumes and smoke from the chimneys, to reduce the amounts of pollution generated by harmful chemicals.

turbine
A shaft (central rod or axle) with a circle of angled blades, like a fan. These spin around when steam or another high-pressure substance blows past them.

vapour
A substance which is in the form of a gas, rather than a liquid or solid, and which can be turned into a liquid by cooling.